MoOn BEArS

MARK NEWMAN

Henry Holt and Company
NEW YORK

Henry Holt and Company, LLC
Publishers since 1866
175 Fifth Avenue
New York, New York 10010
mackids.com

Henry Holt® is a registered trademark of Henry Holt and Company, LLC.

Photographs on pages 6–7 courtesy of Ray Zhu.

Library of Congress Cataloging-in-Publication Data
Newman, Mark, 1946–
Moon bears / Mark Newman.
pages   cm
Audience: Ages 4–8.
ISBN 978-0-8050-9344-5 (hardcover)
1. Asiatic black bear—Juvenile literature. I. Title.
QL737.C27N487 2015   599.78'5–dc23   2014048392

Henry Holt books may be purchased for business or promotional use. For information on bulk purchases, please contact the Macmillan Corporate and Premium Sales Department at (800) 221-7945 x5442 or by e-mail at specialmarkets@macmillan.com.

First Edition—2015
Printed in China by Toppan Leefung Printing Ltd., Dongguan City, Guangdong Province

1 3 5 7 9 10 8 6 4 2

A portion of the proceeds from this book will be donated to Animals Asia Foundation Ltd., a California nonprofit public benefit corporation dedicated to improving the lives of moon bears and all animals in Asia, ending cruelty, and restoring respect for animals Asia-wide. For more information, contact Animals Asia Foundation Ltd., 300 Broadway, Suite 32, San Francisco, CA 94133-4587 [animalsasia.org]. This contribution is not tax-deductible.

*To my sister Wendy, without whom I
would never have made it to Asia to meet
the moon bears and share their story*

The photographs in this book were taken at the Animals Asia Moon Bear Rescue
Centers in Chengdu, China, and Tam Dao, Vietnam. These centers protect bears
that have been rescued from inhumane conditions of captivity and provide an
environment in which they can thrive.

Animals Asia is devoted to improving the welfare of animals in China and
Vietnam. The organization promotes compassion and respect for all animals and
works to bring about long-term change.

To learn more about moon bears and Animals Asia, go to animalsasia.org.

This is Ginny. She's a moon bear.

A moon bear, or Asiatic black bear, gets its name from the large cream-colored crescent across its chest. To some people, this patch of fur looks like the moon. Every moon bear's marking is different.

This is **Angus.**
He's a baby
moon bear.

Moon bears are born tiny and blind. They weigh only about half a pound and are entirely helpless at birth. At four days old, they can walk unsteadily, and after one week, they open their eyes for the first time.

Like all baby bears, moon bear cubs gain weight very quickly from drinking their mother's rich milk. In the wild, their mothers teach them to search for food on their own by the time they are six months old.

Mausi

was born tiny like **Angus** was. But she has grown **big** and **strong**.

Moon bears are fully mature by the time they are four years old. They develop strong claws and leg muscles that allow them to climb trees easily. A moon bear claw can be up to two inches long.

Male moon bears can grow to almost five hundred pounds. Adult females are only about half that weight.

Matilda has a very powerful **nose**. *Sniff, sniff!*

Moon bears have an excellent sense of smell. It is especially useful for locating food and helps them find fruits, nuts, and carrion—dead animals that can serve as a food source. If the wind is right, moon bears can smell one of their favorite treats—honey—from three miles (five kilometers) away.

Poppy's big, round ears help her hear what's happening around her.

A moon bear's hearing is almost as keen as its sense of smell. Some bears, like American black bears, have pointed ears. But moon bears' ears are round and far apart.

Their powerful hearing helps moon bears explore. Moon bears are very intelligent and curious. They investigate every possible nook and cranny, high and low.

Ginny can run **quickly** on **all four legs.**

Moon bears can stand on their back legs quite easily, too.

For a short distance, such as when escaping danger or chasing prey, moon bears can sprint at about thirty miles per hour (forty-eight kilometers per hour). They have been known to walk on their hind legs for up to a quarter mile (0.4 kilometers). Of all the bear species, moon bears are the most comfortable on two legs.

Splash!
Aussie loves water.

Moon bears are excellent swimmers, just like their closest non-bear relatives, the pinnipeds— animals such as seals, sea lions, and walruses.

Mischa loves to climb trees.

When they're not in the water, moon bears often spend time high in the treetops. They climb to hide, to feed, to rest, and even to hibernate inside hollow trees. Moon bears create temporary nests by breaking branches. These nests can be as high as sixty feet (eighteen meters) above the ground.

Mac is omnivorous.

For the most part, moon bears aren't picky eaters—they'll eat whatever they can get their paws on. Their diet is made up mostly of plants. In the spring, moon bears love to munch on tree leaves. They have a sweet tooth, too: They snack on ripe fruit in the summer. In the fall, when nuts are easy to find, moon bears enjoy crunching on acorns, beechnuts, hazelnuts, and walnuts.

Moon bears will eat everything!

They get their protein from a variety of insects, including termites and beetle larvae. If they can catch them, moon bears will also eat small mammals and birds.

Dilly
can be very
noisy.

Moon bears make more kinds of sounds than any other bear. They communicate with at least nine different vocalizations. Female bears "talk" more than males do—they can growl, huff, and scream.

Moon bears can also be quiet.

Like most wild animals, moon bears in the forest try to avoid people. They walk silently and mostly stay hidden during the daytime, becoming active in the evening and at night.

Aussie spends a lot of time relaxing.

In the wild, moon bears rest for long periods of time high up in tree nests. They may even sleep all day, waking only to look for food at dusk. In rescue centers, they may stretch out for hours on a hammock or a swing.

Poppy is from the **northern** part of the **moon bears'** range.

Moon bears' natural habitat covers a large area of Asia. Moon bears in the northern parts of their range hibernate from November to March, usually inside hollow logs, protected by a layer of snow. Because winter food is scarce in the North, moon bears need to hibernate in the colder months.

Matilda is from the southern part.

In the southern part of their range, only pregnant moon bears seek out dens for hibernation. In these regions, food remains available throughout the year, so there's no need to conserve energy by hibernating.

Banjo is naturally solitary.

Moon bears live alone in the wild, except for mothers with cubs. A mother bear usually has two cubs and will keep them with her for two years while she teaches them survival skills.

But under certain conditions, moon bears interact with each other.

When moon bears are brought to rescue centers, they learn to live and play together in groups of as many as twenty bears. Not all bears will get along, but many will form bonds.

Yawn!
Dilly is sleepy.

All that playing and investigating is tiring. The moon bears snuggle in for a good night's sleep. They'll wake up to a new day filled with running, wrestling, snacking, climbing, relaxing, and more!

DID YOU KNOW?

- The bear family includes eight different species: the Asiatic black bear (or moon bear), the American black bear, the brown bear, the polar bear, the giant panda, the sun bear, the sloth bear, and the spectacled bear.

- Typically, a moon bear lives about twenty-five to thirty years in the wild.

- Moon bears are neither nocturnal nor diurnal; they are crepuscular. That is, they are active at dawn and at dusk.

- A moon bear pregnancy is slightly shorter than a human pregnancy; it lasts around eight months. Typically, moon bears give birth to twins in early spring.

- Moon bears communicate with a range of sounds—just like humans! Moon bears have a large vocabulary. They make clucking sounds during play and *tut-tut-tut* sounds in warning.

MORE INFORMATION ABOUT
MOON BEARS

- animalsasia.org

- a-z-animals.com/animals/asian-black-bear

- bearplanet.org/asiatic-blackbear.shtml

Guiberson, Brenda Z. *Moon Bear.* Illustrated by Ed Young. New York: Henry Holt and Company, 2010.

Kvatum, Lia. *Saving Yasha: The Incredible True Story of an Adopted Moon Bear.* Photographs by Liya Pokrovskaya. Washington, DC: National Geographic Society, 2012.

Robinson, Jill, and Marc Bekoff. *Jasper's Story: Saving Moon Bears.* Illustrated by Gijsbert van Frankenhuyzen. Ann Arbor, MI: Sleeping Bear Press, 2013.